The Liberty to Trade as Buttressed by National Law

GEORGE HOWARD EARLE

1890

TABLE OF CONTENTS

INTRODUCTION

For nearly twenty years the national tribunals have been engaged in interpreting the Anti-Trust Act of July 2, 1890. That it has been considered deeply and earnestly by the Supreme Court is shown by the constancy and strength of dissenting opinion.

And yet, when recently asking a number of able and experienced counsel for definite opinions concerning it, they either did not feel able to reply, or did so with the greatest hesitation and difference of view.

Hastily, myself, looking at the cases, I was involved in the same conclusion. The Knight case seemed in direct conflict with the Securities case—four of the Justices thought it was; and the Anderson case with the Montague case. Yet, in later cases, all are equally cited as authority, and often for the same principle. Again: many of the cases speak of the Act as an application of the common law to "national trade" (I mean both interstate and international trade when I use this term), with additional sanctions. Others treat it as going further, but do not say why, or how much.

Then it is decided that "direct" restraints are illegal, "indirect" lawful; but that "indirect" restraints might be "inevitable," while "direct" restraints were often most circuitous. It is confusing to be told that all arrangements tending to stifle competition in national trade are direct and illegal restraints, but that, of course, a partnership that might make such competition even a fraud is, nevertheless, perfectly legal; that "unifications of interest" by complete ownership are indirect and legal, while they are also the most dangerous and illegal forms of direct restraint; that absolutely every restraint of trade is illegal, though there are many exceptions to this rule, without exception; that trade could be "reasonably" restrained, but that nothing could be more "unreasonable" than any restraint of that which is so vital to the nation; that monopolies could only emanate from sovereign authority; but that monopoly merely meant "sole sale," or that which tended to it, no matter how created, etc. Neither was there in text-book nor decision an easy and readily found answer to these apparent enigmas.

It may be that all this presents no difficulty to my brethren of the Bar, but that it did to me cannot be doubted. I am, therefore, tempted by my own difficulties and labors to write this essay, hoping that it may lighten similar ones for others should a solution prove burdensome to them also.

Pressed as I am by other duties, it is not my purpose to write a general treatise upon the subject, but merely to suggest possible solutions and explanations of some of the main difficulties of the subject including, of course, those already referred to.

THE SHERMAN ACT

(1) What restraints of national trade do the Anti-Trust Acts make illegal? (2) What monopolies are condemned by them?

The wording of the Sherman Act is clear and comprehensive. It reads: "Every contract, combination, or conspiracy;" "every person who shall monopolize or attempt to monopolize," and "any part of the trade." etc.

This is certainly broad enough. It says nothing about "reasonable restraints," or "indirect restraints" being excepted; though the Supreme Court has consequently held that "reasonable restraints were not excepted, while, nevertheless, "indirect restraints" were!

This may seem serious and illogical, but, to anticipate a little, it is not, being but a matter of confusing terminology.

Whether serious or not, it is as to ultimate results, and a clear understanding, exceedingly important to determine (1) whether the Act really makes all restraints of trade illegal; and (2) whether, if so, it in this respect exceeds the common law.

The unhesitating reply is, that, regarding substance, and not mere nomenclature, the Act both says and means "every;" and that in so saying and meaning it but applies the rule of the common law to the Nation's efforts to protect its own trade.

This statement can hardly go unchallenged, in view of many opinions of the Supreme Court itself; but it is really not matter difficult of explanation.

Until the Freight Association case it had generally been conceded that, as stated by Mr. Justice Jackson, In re Greene, 52 Fed. (1892), "when Congress * * * adopts or creates common law offences, the court may properly look to that body of jurisprudence for the true meaning and definition of such crimes, if they are not clearly defined in the act creating them. * * * The act does not undertake to define what constitutes a contract, combination or conspiracy in restraint of trade, and recourse

7

must, therefore, be had to the common law for the proper definition of these general terms, and to ascertain whether the acts charged come within the statute;" or, as Chief Justice Fuller more succinctly said in the Knight case: "It was in the light of well settled principles that the Act of July 2, 1890, was framed." This conclusion is fortified by the many authorities cited in the opinion of the Court of Appeals in the Freight Association case. In the last-named case, a combining and conspiring body of railroads, asserting that what they did was legal at common law, invoked this principle in the Court of Appeals, and, succeeding in convincing that court that their view of the common law was correct, won their case. On appeal, therefore, it was open to the Supreme Court to reverse, either because the common law did include the offense complained of, or because the statute exceeded the common law; and, as it was convinced that, in any event, the purpose of the Act had been invaded, it selected the simpler course of "assuming" that the common law did not include the offence, but that, even so, the statute did. And so originated a doctrine that bas caused much discussion and some difficulties—to be later mentioned.

The Supreme Court, after referring to Mogul vs. McGregor et al., cited by the courts below as holding that contracts in reasonable restraint of trade were legal at common law, continues: "But, assuming that agreements of this nature are not void at common law, and that the various cases cited by the learned courts below show it, the answer to the statement of their validity now is to be found in the terms of the statute under consideration." And this language is again quoted in Loewe vs. Lawlor. This assumption, once made, has been, since, continued as fully serving the purpose; but as it has resulted in making the law self-contradictory in other cases, and introduced difficulty and confusion, it is of great importance to inquire whether it was well founded—an inquiry still open if I be right—and thus to ascertain whether the common law has not already solved the difficulties thus arising.

Let us, then, inquire whether the common law did not also make every contract, combination and conspiracy in restraint of trade unlawful?

The true distinction lies in the difference between restraining trade and restraining men from engaging in trade. This is often lost sight of, but it is none the less a real and substantial distinction.

The law, unquestionably, protected the liberty of citizen or subject to engage in trade from wrongful molestation; but it did not protect it absolutely. It might always, for example, from the earliest times, be made valueless by an exercise of a like liberty by others—that is, by competition.

But it was protected from all unlawful attack, absolutely. It was only thus protected as part of the liberty of the citizen, and the liberty to make a binding contract might be equally important. There was, therefore, an inherent and inevitable conflict between these two phases of man's liberty:

the liberty to bind himself, that is, to contract, and the liberty to remain unbound —the right to contract pro tanto and of necessity destroying the other right. This balance being even—liberty against liberty—public policy had to control the issue; and trade, being of vital interest to the public, the contractor was permitted to choose his freedom to contract wherever such choice advanced trade. That is the whole doctrine of "reasonable restraints," if the best considered cases are looked to. In other words, if the contract were fair and reasonable, and beneficial to the public—that is, in advancement of an enlarged trade—it was "reasonable" to permit a liberty of contract which, if denied, would tend to diminish trade. "Reasonable" restraints of trade, therefore, were not in reality, restraints upon trade at all, but only such voluntary restraints upon traders as advanced trade; and it was chiefly because they advanced trade that they were permitted. While the law was tender of the rights of the individual, and protected them in trade, its chief end and aim was totality—trade in gross, the trade of the nation or realm; and of that it was jealous to the extreme.

Sir F. Pollock (citing Leather Cloth Co. vs. Lorsont) says: "The admission of limited restrictions is commonly spoken of as an exception to the general policy of the law. But it seems better to regard it rather as another branch of it. Restriction which is reasonable * * * is allowed by the very same policy that forbids restrictions generally, and for like reasons."

Again, in Rannie vs. Irvine, Maule, J., says with fine succinctness: "The exception is in furtherance of the rule."

In Homer vs. Ashford, Best, C. J., says: "The first object of the law is to promote the public interest; the second to preserve the rights of individuals;" and then, after denouncing restraints of trade, he again gives the true reason for allowing "partial" or "reasonable" restraints of it: "The effect of such contracts is to encourage rather than cramp."

Again, in the leading case of Mallan vs. May, unanimously approved by eight judges in the Exchequer Chamber in Price vs. Greene, Baron Parke, whose explanations are always so clear, says: "The rule * * * is, that total restraints of trade, which the law so favors, are absolutely bad, and that all restraints, though only partial, if nothing more appear, are presumed to be bad. * * * Contracts in restraint of trade are in themselves, if nothing show them to be reasonable, bad in the eye of the law. * * * But if there are circumstances recited in the instrument (or, probably, if they appear by averment) it is for the court to determine whether the contract be a fair and reasonable one or not; and the test appears to be, whether it be prejudicial or not to the public interest; for it is on grounds of public policy alone that these contracts are supported or avoided. * * * It is justly observed by Lord Wynford that the effect of those contracts" (those allowed) "is to encourage rather than cramp the employment of capital in trade, and the promotion of industry." And, finally, Lord Macnaghten, speaking in the House of Lords and so settling the law of England, says in Nordenfelt vs. Maxim: "The public have an interest in every person carrying on his trade freely; so has the individual. All interference with individual liberty of action, in trading, and all restraints of trade of themselves, if there is nothing more, are contrary to public policy, and, therefore, void. That is the general rule. But, there are exceptions. * * * It is a sufficient justification and, indeed, it is the only justification, if the restriction is reasonable—reasonable, that is, in reference to the interests of the parties concerned, and reasonable in reference to the interests of the public—so framed and so guarded as to afford adequate protection to the party in whose interest it is imposed, while, at the same time, it is in no way injurious to the public." Finally, in the Addyston case: "The inhibition against restraints of trade at common law seems, at first, to have had no exceptions. * * * After a time it became apparent to the people and the courts that it was in the interest of trade that certain covenants in restraint should be enforced. It was of importance, as an incentive to industry and honest dealing in trade." If it be asked of what importance all this is, in view of the fact that the Supreme Court has, in any event, already held that every contract in restraint of trade is void, the reply is, that if the so-called reasonable restraints of the common law, properly understood, are to be included, the Act is then defeating its own purpose of protecting and encouraging national trade; for, if they be included, then are contracts in furtherance of trade made illegal. But a second and greater difficulty lies in the fact that, driven just as the common law judges were by the real reason and sense of the thing the courts are one by one allowing all these alleged exceptions to a professedly universal rule, and thus making both the rule and the exceptions uncertain to those who do not inquire deeply. It is believed that the court has never precluded itself by this labor-saving assumption from making this inquiry, and that the inquiry when made will only fortify the conclusion that it has reached independently, while at the same time clarifying the principle governing the so-called exceptions.

The court, in any event, has never said that any restraint or limitation of the totality of National trade was a reasonable thing to permit, though it has already permitted an exercise of the liberty of contract that tended to its advancement; but that is the exact position of the common law.

MONOPOLIES

In respect to these, the Act again uses the word "every." "Every person who shall monopolize or attempt to monopolize, and it is not all, but "any part of the trade, etc.

What is it that the Act again denounces "every person" for either doing or attempting? What does "monopoly" really mean? What evil did it inflict? Why was it prohibited?

Mr. Justice Jackson says in In re Greene: "A monopoly, in the prohibitive sense, involves the "element of an exclusive privilege or grant which restrained others from the exercise of a right or liberty which they had before the monopoly was "secured," and gives many other meanings.

It is manifest, however, that Congress in these United States, and in the year 1890, was not legislating against the monopolies that bad been destroyed by the statute of James in 1623!

There is no doubt that, since the statute of James, to unlawfully exclude one from competing with you in trade is to monopolize; but it seems impossible that the word was not also used in the Act of Congress, in its primary, natural and simplest meaning. The real evil is aptly described by the exact meaning of the word monopoly, that is, "to sell alone." That power gave a right of taxing and oppressing the whole nation, only limited by its means and necessities! Then why was not the meaning of the word just what it naturally meant? Why should it not be construed as prohibiting the power of "sole sale" or "sole purchase" in national commerce? Is it not an evil that a single person or combination can regulate every interstate transaction in a necessity of life, thus usurping the power of Congress in that respect totally and completely? The question is but asked. Mr. Justice Peckham so thinks: "Nor is it for the substantial interests of the country that any one commodity should be within the sole power and subject to the sole will of one powerful combination of capital."

The industry and ability of Professor Stimson ("Federal and State Constitutions") excludes at least one reason for negative answer, and the statute of James another.

"Sole buying, selling, making, working or using of anything" was certainly denounced by that statute. It is asserted that the common law only prohibited these, as explained by Lord Coke, when resulting from exclusive grants, etc. But that is not so.

As demonstrated by Professor Stimson, the trade of the middle ages being controlled by corporations, or guilds, restraints, then, were generally by so-called "ordinances" or "by-laws;" and these were prohibited by a declaratory statute in 1436, the statute being against by-laws in restraint of trade, "by persons in confederacy for their singular profit and the common damage of the people." This statute was again reënacted in 1503. That such monopolies were illegal in the time of James is also shown by Lord Coke's own argument and the decision in Devenant's case. In denouncing monopolies, Parliament and courts, and Coke himself, perfectly familiar with the law, confined themselves not to those which alone were admittedly illegal, but only to those whose illegality was still contested—exclusive grants by the sovereign. The contest was not at all whether lesser powers could inflict the curse of "sole sale" upon the people. It was settled long before, that they could not; but whether the sovereign power itself could still do so.

Professor Stimson seems thoroughly to establish this. But beyond this it is now settled by In re Debs, the Addyston case, and Loewe vs. Lawlor that whatever is prohibited to sovereign States is likewise and a fortiori unlawful in mere aggregations of individuals. Finally, that "monopolies," in their modern sense, hark back to their natural and original common law sense as applied to "unifications," etc. See Mr. Justice McKenna's opinion, National vs. Texas: "Unified tactics with regard to prices"—the exact results of "sole sale" seven hundred years before!

But if this be so, why should not the general rule as to "tendency" constituting the offence, be applicable? This would certainly seem worthy of consideration, especially as it makes this provision a vital and useful part of the statute? If one person or group control the whole of a necessary commodity throughout the United States, there is not merely the "power and interest" necessary to create the tendency constituting illegality in other cases; but there is absolute necessity that he or it must regulate interstate transactions in that commodity. In view of the investigations of Professor Stimson, as well as the actual decision in National vs. Texas, it is not difficult to say what the ultimate conclusion will be.

In the Securities case Mr. Justice Holmes says: "There is a natural feeling that somehow or other the statute meant to strike at combinations great enough to cause just anxiety on the part of those who love their country more than money, while it viewed such little ones as I have supposed with just indifference. This notion, it may be said, somehow breathes from the pores of the Act, although it seems to be contradicted in every way by the words in detail. And it has occurred to me that it might be that when a combination reached a certain size it might have attributed to it more of the character of a monopoly merely by virtue of its size." And the test of Mr. Justice Jackson of "exclusion of others" evidently created great difficulty in Mr. Justice Holmes's mind. But if, as has been shown, the fundamental offence was "sole sale" or attempts to reach it, tendency to it; and exclusion by sovereign or other authority was but a single and, indeed, last phase of it, is not Mr. Justice Holmes's feeling fully supported by the very words of the Act? He says, at page 403: "Much trouble is made by substituting other phrases assumed to be equivalent, which then are reasoned from as if they were in the Act." And is not this difficulty here the result of substituting "attempts to exclude others" for the wider phrase "sole sale"? The other difficulties are answered in National vs. Texas: "To contend for these extremes is to overlook the difference in the effect of actions, and to limit too much the function and power of government. By arguing from extremes almost every exercise of government can be shown to be a deprivation of individual liberty." Reading of Mr. Justice Holmes' natural feeling, I could not but think of Lord Bramwell's dictum regarding the "feelings" of great lawyers, 13 Ap. C. 12, "the four judges were great lawyers, and I believe that a great lawyer may be, as it were, instinctively right, without at the moment being able to give a good reason for his opinion." In prohibiting monopolies, and attempts at monopoly, Congress and the common law never intended or could have intended to prohibit necessary and useful things that in their nature had to be to some extent monopolies. Two towns unconnected by a railroad were certainly not forbidden to have a railroad because a railroad would, in a sense, be a monopoly. What was and has always been the evil was substituting for "competition," where that was either established or naturally and ordinarily possible, "sole sale" or "unified tactics" as to prices, and not at all to prevent the starting of a new industry. And that this was the intent of the common law and statute of James declaring it is shown by the reservation of right to grant patents for new inventions. The policy was to encourage industry, and that answers such objections. In many phases of the matter "magnitude" is, as the word implies, the very gist of it, and the dangerous measure, as in many other cases, must be found through the sound sense of the tribunal deciding it. An ordinary partnership, an ordinary consolidation of two butchers, out of the thousands in New York City or the United States, can in nothing but a finespun impracticable sense, unfit for a basis of any sound jurisprudence, be said to constitute a monopoly, or a tendency to monopoly; although, without doubt, Mr. Justice Holmes was right in holding that the combination in United States vs. Swift was illegal. An "overshadowing combination" necessarily gives the power and necessary interest to inflict the evils flowing from "sole sale," while the evil may easily be totally wanting in many minor and convenient combinations which really facilitate trade. In construing every statute since Heydon's case, "what was the evil and effect" has always been carefully scrutinized. And in this matter "the evils" were "the effects" naturally flowing from the prohibited "sole sale," and not necessarily the mere method of accomplishing the prohibited thing which, however created, always and almost inevitably inflicted the evils.

INTENT

The Anti-Trust Act, being a criminal as well as remedial statute, intent is, of course, necessary. But it is also, of course, only intent as legally defined.

As Mr. Justice Holmes so felicitously puts it in Ellis vs. United States: "If a man intentionally adopts certain conduct in certain circumstances known to him, and that conduct is forbidden by the law under those circumstances he intentionally breaks the law in the only sense in which the law ever considers intent."

But there is another viewpoint of importance in this connection, which, in its ultimate results, becomes vital, and that is that from which the law ascertains or presumes an intent as to results flowing from the forbidden acts. It was long since said: "Thought is not triable," but quite as long ago that "actions speak louder than words;" and it may be added that a knowledge of human nature as loudly as either.

When we pass, then, from proved acts, and an inquiry as to the ends sought through them becomes necessary, the legal method is well established, though it has a duality of expression that is sometimes confusing. It may either be said that intent is conclusively presumed under certain circumstances, or that intent is of no importance whatever. But the latter expression is sometimes misleading, as, while in some cases it may be of no importance, in others it is the vital, determinative fact!

To explain this further: An act is done from which certain results naturally, reasonably, or ordinarily may be expected. Then it is perfectly proper to say, as the Earl of Halsbury, L. C., does in South Wales Miners' Federation vs. Glamorgan:

"It is, further, a principle of the law, applicable even to the criminal law, that people are presumed to intend the reasonable consequences of their acts." Indeed, this presumption is so absolutely necessary that the Supreme

Court has had to apply it even to the enactments of the sovereign States themselves, so interpreting their statutory acts, no matter how they themselves assert their purposes. "In whatever language a statute may be framed, its purpose must be determined by its natural and reasonable effects. * * * The motives of the legislators, considered as the purposes they had in view, will always be presumed to be to accomplish that which follows as the natural and reasonable effect of their enactments." And, in such a case, it is equally accurate to say intent is immaterial; but this may well mislead, and has often misled where proof of intent becomes essential, as it sometimes really does in these cases.

This is best illustrated by the cases themselves. Mr. Justice Peckham says: "It is useless for the defendants to say they did not intend to regulate or affect interstate commerce. They intended to make the very combination and agreement which they in fact did make, and they must be held to have intended (if in such case intention is of the least importance) the necessary and direct result of their agreement."

So Mr. Justice Harlan says in the Securities case: "Is the motive with which a forbidden combination or conspiracy was formed at all material when it appears that the necessary tendency of the particular combination or conspiracy in question is to restrict or suppress free competition?" etc.

On the other hand, Mr. Justice Holmes says, in the Swift case: "The statute gives this proceeding against combinations in restraint of commerce among the States and against attempts to monopolize the same. Intent is almost essential to such a combination, and is essential to such an attempt."

There is, of course, no conflict in these opinions; and reading them together there should be no danger of misunderstanding or confusion. But I have known lawyers who argued that intent was immaterial, as well as those who argued that it must be independently proved. Of course, as a rule, both were wrong, for intent is always material in some sense, though inferable from the acts themselves; while, on the other hand, there are cases where, it not being reasonably inferable from the facts of the alleged conspiracy, it is necessary in some legitimate way to establish it to constitute the offence at all.

Lord Watson states this clearly in Allen vs. Flood, 1898 A. C. 102: "The object of an act, that is the results which will necessarily or naturally follow from the circumstances, in which it is committed, may give it a wrongful character, but it ought not to be confounded with the motive of the actor. To discharge a loaded gun is, in many circumstances, a perfectly harmless proceeding; to fire it on a highway, in front of a restive horse, might be a very different matter."

This will be further considered in the next chapter.

TENDENCY AND POWER

Around these terms and "competition" has been fought the chief battle in this country for the freedom of man in relation to trade.

Where a result is considered seriously detrimental it has been the uniform policy of the common law to enforce the doctrine that men should not lead or be led into temptation to bring it to pass. And, if the application of it did not originate in cases of restraints, it was certainly very early applied in them. The declaratory statute of James equally prohibits that which "tends" as that which constitutes "sole sale."

The general doctrine has never been more clearly enunciated than in the leading case of Egerton vs. Earl Brownlow, where Lord Brougham says: "But the law * * * taking security against the infirmity of human nature regards the tendency, as well as the act, and removes the motives to offending that it may not have to punish the offence."

Lord Truro, at page 199: "I repeat that what may occur in the particular instance is not the point; it is the general tendency."

And Lord St. Leonards, at page 235: "It is a dangerous power to be placed in the hands of any man with such a temptation to use it—a temptation almost irresistible. God forbid that I should say there are not men who could resist it; but the temptation is more than you are justified in laying before a man; more than you are justified in exposing him to. You are not justified in raising so fearful an issue."

The "tendency," then, which the law regards, is tendency to wrong from that which really tempts to its perpetration. Not mere possibility or power; but such possibility or power as, taking human nature as it is, supply such temptation as to create a dangerous probability of some yielding to and committing the offence.

This, then, being the doctrine, it may easily be seen that "power" without interest, or, if you please, temptation, to restrain is not necessarily illegal.

While on the one hand, under some circumstances, "power" may constitute a deadly threat to public interests, on the other it may be innocuous, or even largely beneficial. "Power," therefore, when spoken of as constituting the offence, must always be understood as power coupled with actual intent, or interest, or temptation, to restrain; but that is "tendency." And not only is "tendency" to restrain, to monopolize, denounced by the act of James, but, as Chief Justice Fuller points out in the Knight case: "All the authorities agree that, in order to vitiate a contract or combination it is not essential that its result should be a complete monopoly; it is sufficient if it really tends to that end, and to deprive the public of the advantages which flow from free competition."

The Knight case so strongly demonstrates the danger of holding that power alone does constitute tendency or the consequent illegality, that nothing more need be said on that subject; but that those who intentionally conspire to restrain national trade are within the Act is plain, though none of their acts without such intent would have amounted to tendency. He who does, with intent of accomplishing a given result, is certainly estopped from denying that what he did tended to that which he intended that it should tend to.

Sir F. Pollock well says: "It does not lie in a man's mouth to say that the consequence which he deliberately planned and procured is too remote for the law to treat as a consequence. The iniquity of such a defence is obvious in the gross examples of the criminal law. Commanding, procuring, or inciting to a murder cannot have any 'legal consequences,' the act of compliance or obedience being a crime; but no one has suggested, on this ground, any doubt that procurement is also a crime." As will be seen, an intended restraint must always be a "direct" restraint, and no matter how indirect the means of accomplishment.

To summarize: To constitute an offence within the Act there must have been either the intent to commit the offence, or to commit acts, or acquire power tending to it; but "power" alone does not constitute the offence.

Two quotations by the Chief Justice from opinions by Mr. Justice Holmes must ever be kept in view:

"If, as we must assume, the scheme is entertained, it is, of course, contrary to the very words of the statute. * * * It is suggested that the several acts charged are lawful and that intent can make no difference. But they are bound together as part of a single plan. The plan may make the parts unlawful. * * * The statute is directed against a series of acts, and acts of several, the acts of combining, with intent to do other acts. 'The very plot is an act in itself.' But an act, which in itself is merely a voluntary muscular contraction, derives all its character from the consequences which will follow it under the circumstances in which it was done. When the acts consist of making a combination calculated to cause temporal damage, the power to punish such acts, when done maliciously, cannot be denied because they are to be followed and worked out by conduct which might have been lawful if not preceded by the acts. No conduct has such an absolute privilege as to justify all possible schemes of which it may be a part. The most innocent and constitutionally protected of acts or omissions may be made a step in a criminal plot, and if it is a step in a plot, neither its innocence nor the constitution is sufficient to prevent the punishment of the plot by law."

The law is a practical science, and by "tendency" it means something real, something, as Mr. Justice Holmes puts it, which amounts to "dangerous probability." As he so well says (Swift case, 196 U. S. 396): "Where acts are not sufficient in themselves to produce a result which the law seeks to prevent—for instance, the monopoly—but require further acts in addition to the mere forces of Nature to bring that result to pass, an intent to bring it to pass is necessary in order to produce a dangerous probability that it will happen. Commonwealth vs. Peaslee, 177 Massachusetts 267, 272. But when that intent and the consequent dangerous probability exist, this statute, like many others, and like the common law in some cases, directs itself against that dangerous probability, as well as against the complete result." Of course this intent must be proved and inferred, as in other cases, from conduct. Unlawful acts, invasions of liberty, limiting of discretion, the creation of such a temptation as would naturally lead to it; but, however established, when once formed, and followed by action, the offence is established; for intent, being intensified tendency, the offence has appeared, the danger to society has arisen!

INDIRECTNESS OF RESTRAINT

One would think, in reading some of the briefs submitted on behalf of the trusts, that "indirectness of restraint" was a mere arbitrary unmeaning phrase solely devised that a trust could make some pretense of a defence in the absence of all real ones, whereas it means little more than the absence of dangerous probability explained by Mr. Justice Holmes. So, it is the present purpose to inquire not merely whether this be so, but whether it is not, indeed, but an abbreviation covering one of the most essential and scientifically thought out doctrines of the law.

If the doctrine, in this connection, be understood, it may be defined as the effort of the law so to limit the doctrine of tendency as to prevent its improper extension to the extinguishment of all other rights, or "the doctrine of indirection defines the limitations of the doctrine of 'tendency' so that all rights and powers may not be absorbed by an absurd extension of the latter."

The first and most important thing to be remembered in this connection is that the doctrine has no application whatever to tortious or involuntarily suffered restraints, its sole application being to cases of voluntary or contractual restraint, involving in its accomplishment no wrongful means or end. This is constantly overlooked in argument, and leads but to confusion and error. The doctrine of "tendency," indeed, if properly understood and limited, comprises the whole doctrine of "indirectness" within itself.

Sir Frederick Pollock, in "Contracts," page 317, discussing Egerton vs. Earl Brownlow, 4 H. of L. C. 1 (1853), says: "The question * * * was whether there was an apparent tendency to mischief * * * or only a remote possibility of inconvenient consequences. * * * Egerton vs. Earl Brownlow, however, is certainly a cardinal authority for one rule which applies in all cases of 'public policy,' namely, that the tendency of the transaction at the time, not its actual result, must be looked to." This con- trasting "tendency" with "remote possibility" is inherent in the subject, and must have at all times and in all such cases been a necessary part of the mental processes of the courts; but it is remarkable how little prominence it attained before the Nation undertook to protect national trade, and thus required a consideration of State as contrasted with national rights. It is confidently believed that even if the term "indirect" in connection with restraints of trade was ever used in the whole history of the common law, its use or discussion in one thousand years has not equaled either, under the Anti Trust Act since 1895. Indeed, until I found the passage in Pollock, just quoted, I had no reference to the principle at common law, and, even there, the term is not used and the discussion is but as to "tendency." This advantage would have been gained, from so confining the discussion, that it would not have required all the labor of defining and restricting the enunciation of a new term of art. And it is submitted that the doctrine enunciated in the Egerton case, and by Mr. Justice Holmes, as just quoted, was all that was necessary, and would have led to the same results. Indeed, he makes it the differentiating factor between the Knight and Swift cases, saying, at page 397 of the latter: "Moreover, it is a direct object, it is that for the sake of which the specific acts and courses of conduct are done and adopted. Therefore the case is not like The United States vs. E. C. Knight Co., 156 U. S. 1." No more illuminating or better exposition of those cases could be found!

One thing is certain, and that is that this unhappy word is intended to enunciate no new doctrine in controversion of the maxim: "Dolus circuitu non purgatur," and one of the chief objections to the word "direct," in this connection, is that in other connections it is used as an equivalent of "proximate," and so suggests an inquiry along that line. But this cannot be correct, as a power may be "inevitable," at least in some sense, certainly "foreseeable" in its results, and not be "direct" at all (see the Knight case), and yet be one that may never be reached, or if reached, be so by the most circuitous path possible, and be "direct." In the Knight case a complete control of manufactories, in every respect and as to every discretion, was secured; and yet the restraint was held to be "indirect," "remote;" while in the Addyston case but a limited amount of discretion was yielded, and yet, because that yielding might, through many possible steps, end ultimately in a decrease of national trade, the restraint was held to be "direct" and unlawful. But the court found conduct evincing intent and consequent dangerous probability in the later case, and thought it lacking, on the evidence, in the former!

The Knight and Securities cases afford a much stronger instance. Unification by complete ownership took place in both instances. So complete was the analogy that four of the justices held that the law laid down in the former case was overruled by the latter; and yet, on the facts found, identical acts, found in the one case as constituting indirect methods of restraint, were, in the other, found to be direct; and on no question of law did the latter case depart from the former! Both cases are constantly cited by the Supreme Court to justify a single doctrine, and correctly. As has been indicated, the reason is that while the acquisition of "power" to restrain may be viewed with such just suspicion as to make it prima facie dangerous, illegal, to require explanation, that still, if that explanation satisfy the court that there was neither purpose nor interest amounting to dangerous temptation to misapply it, the justly and lawfully acquired power can be lawfully retained; because neither restraint nor the power acquired with interest or intent to restrain exists, necessary to constitute that tendency, which is equally illegal with restraint itself.

To repeat: The doctrine of "direct" or "indirect" restraints would have continued to be explained, as at common law, by a sensible definition of the term tendency, had not the doctrine for identical reasons become so important a one in solving questions resulting from the duality of government and powers in the United States; but having been necessarily so used in regard to such questions generally, it most naturally was also applied to them in this particular respect, as to a national matter. Nevertheless, the common law doctrine of "tendency," properly understood, also fully covered the subject.

As the purpose is to consider the Knight case separately in this connection, what has been said will only be justified shortly here. But first, a word of caution. It is not the purpose of this essay to justify the findings of fact of that case, the inference of interest or tendency; and tendency is a question of fact of any particular case. Such findings, however important to the particular case, are of no importance to any one else, binding neither juries nor the court itself, in later cases. This has been ably pointed out in a restraint case where the inferences of fact of another restraint case, previously passed upon by it, were again unsuccessfully urged upon the House of Lords. An exact parallel of the Knight and Securities cases, in America!

And, in addition to this, it must never be forgotten that while the law remains and should be permanent, that conditions of civilization and trade are constantly changing; and that it was held under prior conditions, that certain conduct did not tend to restraint; still, under subsequent ones, it is permissible to hold that tendency may be clear even from identical conduct. So that identically opposite decisions may only demonstrate the unchangeable quality of the law's hostility to restraints of prosperity, however brought about. For the present, but two opinions will be referred to, as it is thought they perfectly clarify the subject—Mr. Justice Peckham's, in the Anderson case, and Mr. Justice White's, in the Securities case, the latter because no stronger view can possibly be contended for than that of the minority, which dissented because the majority would not go even so far.

In the Anderson case, then, the doctrine is thus lucidly stated: "Where the subject-matter of the agreement does not directly relate to and act upon and embrace interstate commerce, and where the undisputed facts clearly show that the purpose of the agreement was not to regulate, obstruct, or restrain that commerce, but that it was entered into with the object of properly and fairly regulating the transaction of the business in which the parties to the agreement were engaged, such agreement will be upheld as not within the statute, where it can be seen that the character and terms of the agreement are well calculated to attain the purpose for which it was formed; and where the effect of its formation and enforcement upon interstate trade or commerce is, in any event but indirect and incidental, and not its purpose or object. As is said in Smith vs. Alabama: 'There are many cases, however, where the acknowledged powers of a State may be exerted and applied in such a manner as to affect foreign or interstate commerce without being intended to operate as commercial regulations.' The same is true as to certain kinds of agreements entered into between persons engaged in the same business for the direct and bona fide purpose of properly and reasonably regulating the conduct of their business among themselves and with the public. If an agreement of that nature, while apt and proper for the purpose thus intended, should possibly, though only indirectly and unintentionally, affect interstate trade or commerce, in that event we think the agreement would be good. Otherwise, there is scarcely any agreement among men which has interstate or foreign commerce for its subject that may not remotely be said to in some obscure way affect that commerce, and be void." The synonyms of "indirect," used in this decision, being "unintended," "obscure," "not its purpose," "incidentally," "possibly though unintentionally," "if at all," "no purpose of affecting or in any manner restraining," "if at all only in a very indirect and remote," "no direct tendency to diminish or in any way impede or restrain," "no tendency directly or indirectly to restrict competition," "not with intent or purpose of affecting in the slightest degree," "no tendency to limit the extent of the demand, or to limit the number marketed, or to limit or reduce price, or place any impediment in the course of the commercial stream," "too remote and fanciful," "reasonable and fair," "possibly in but a remote way." But what is this, but an able application of the common law, as laid down by Baron Parke in Mallan vs. May?

In the Securities case, Mr. Justice White says: "Where an authority is exerted by a State, which is within its power, and that authority, as exercised, does not touch interstate commerce or its instrumentalities, and can only have an effect upon such commerce by reason of the reflex and remote results of the exertion of the lawful power, it cannot be said, without a contradiction in terms that the power exercised is a regulation, because a direct burden upon commerce * * * The question whether a burden is direct and therefore constitutes a regulation of interstate commerce is to be determined by ascertaining whether the power exerted is lawful, generally speaking, and then by finding whether its exercise in the particular case was such as to cause it to be illegal, because directly burdening interstate commerce. If in a given case the power be lawful and the mode in which it is exercised be not such as to directly burden, there is no regulation of commerce, although as an indirect result of the exertion of the lawful power some effect may be produced upon commerce." But, of course, the mere fact that a result merely "may be produced" and as "an indirect result" cannot even at common law amount to the "dangerous probability" constituting "tendency" with which the law deals.

Or, in a nutshell, as is said by the same justice in Pabst vs. Crenshaw: "The distinction between direct and indirect burdens upon interstate commerce, by means of which the harmonious working of our constitutional system has been made possible."

But, of course, it must not be forgotten, as already pointed out, that no exercise of power is lawful if used to accomplish an illegal purpose, or that really tends to the accomplishment of it, or the public evil involved in its accomplishment. But, assuming that the application of the power is for a lawful purpose and with lawful tendencies, its merely possible results are not controlling. But the distinction between "tendency" or "intent," and mere "unintended possibility," must ever be kept in mind if error is to be avoided. And it is to be feared that it is not always.

A very satisfactory way of stating and explaining this is that of Chief Justice Marshall, in Gibbons vs. Ogden, as is so ably pointed out by Mr. Justice Moody in the Employers' Liability cases.

Where there are two powers, one in the State, another in the nation, one in individuals, or another in the nation, the exercise of the one power is not to be destroyed by the mere existence of the other, where that exercise is bona fide, with no intent or purpose of invading, or manifest, or natural tendency to invade it. In such cases there must be temptation added to power to constitute tendency, or that intent that is, of course, its equivalent, or most intensified form.

It is worth while to repeat that: "Where acts are not sufficient in themselves to produce a result which the law seeks to prevent, for instance, the monopoly" (or, of course, that which tends to it), "but require further acts in addition to the mere forces of nature to bring that result to pass, an intent to bring it to pass is necessary in order to produce a dangerous probability that it will happen. But when that intent and the consequent dangerous probability exist, this statute, like many others, and like the common law in some cases, directs itself against that dangerous probability as well as against the completed result."

But it must also be borne in mind that, as trade is carried on for profit, and rarely successfully by the pure altruist, the acquirement of power that offers its owner unlimited opportunities of attaining the object—profit—and satisfying cupidity, but at the expense of the consuming public, needs no additions "to the mere forces of nature to bring that result to pass." "Tendency" has appeared, and with it unlawfulness.

INDIRECTNESS IN RELATION TO CASES OF NON-ASSENT

It is manifest from what has been said, that this doctrine of indirectness can but apply to cases of assent. Lacking assent you have mere torts, invasions of right; and in such cases the doctrine of the maxim "dolus circuitu non purgatur" applies in full force.

It is a striking fact that in no such case has the Supreme Court ever denied a citizen redress for an invasion of his constitutional right and election to engage in national trade!

The acquirement of power by unlawful means, or the unlawful use of it in such manner as possibly to affect the Nation's rights in its trade, never overcomes the prima facie presumption of illegality always arising in such cases. Good purposes are not legally to be deduced from bad purposes or evil acts.

The doctrine of "indirectness," resting upon the lawfulness of what is done, can have no relevancy whatever to that which is in any way unlawfully done—to any tort or conspiracy! When people begin to do unlawful things that may injure national trade, there is always enough "dangerous probability" for the law to interfere at once. "Indirectness" meaning, in this connection, nothing more than "mere unintended possibility from lawful exercise through lawful means, of lawful rights or powers," an intended restraint upon trade itself must be illegal. It is illegal to strive to destroy, in any degree, that upon which public welfare depends. It makes no difference how indirect the means adopted, how lawful in themselves. Acts, any acts done in furtherance of a conspiracy to restrain are illegal. A plot to restrain National trade is a direct invasion of the express words of the Act, is as "direct" an invasion as anything can be, and "indirectness" of any or all means cannot make that which is itself direct, unlawful; indirect and legal; nor can they change what is expressly in itself denounced as criminal, into the pure and innocent, though the trusts frequently attempt to make them do so!

This is fully expressed by Judge Woods in the much-commended opinion in U. S. vs. Debs:

"A conspiracy, to be sure, consists in an agreement to do something, but in the sense of the law and therefore in the sense of this statute, it must be an agreement between two or more to do by concerted action something criminal or unlawful, or, it may be, to do something lawful by criminal or unlawful means. A conspiracy, therefore, is in itself unlawful, and, in so far as this statute is directed against conspiracies in restraint of trade among the several States, it is not necessary to look for the illegality of the offence in the kind of restraint proposed; and since it would be unnecessary it would be illogical. * * * Any proposed restraint of trade, though it be in itself innocent, if it is to be accomplished by conspiracy, is unlawful."

Again, Judge Taft says, in Thomas vs. Company: "The breach of a contract is unlawful; a combination with that as its purpose is unlawful, and is a conspiracy; * * * therefore, this combination was for an unlawful purpose and is a conspiracy within the statute."

And so it was also determined in the Addyston case: "Another aspect of this contract of association brings it within the term used in the statute, 'a conspiracy in restraint of trade.' * * * One of the means adopted by the defendants * * * was * * * illegal and fraudulent. * * * No matter what the excuse for the combination by defendants in restraint of trade, the illegality of the means stamps it as a conspiracy, and so brings it within that term of the Federal statute."

It results that, while it has for manifest reasons been necessary to carefully scrutinize intent and tendency when all that has been done was to exercise a lawful power in lawful manner, and thus to exclude "tendency" from the mere possession of such power unaccompanied by temptation or proved intent to misuse, there is no such reason in the case of wrongdoers, that they may be left free to exploit the public. Where illegal conduct is thought necessary, innocence of ultimate purpose need not and is not assumed; nor does public policy require that the State should run any risk of the possibility being converted into accomplished injury. Everything is to be presumed against such wrong-doers; and full precaution is justifiable that the public may not suffer. While the probabilities of lawful conduct may be confined to beneficial results, the probability of crime is injury. For crime is not resorted to where "legitimate means and lawful methods" will suffice. In any event, no public policy can require the taking of any chances in favor of such wrong-doers.

COMPETITION

Competition does represent, not the productive forces of trade, but only its police. Unfortunately, it is none the less necessary, on that account. Civilization is but a curtailment of competition, a substitution of coöperation for universal strife and enmity. To say, therefore, that a restraint of competition is equivalent to a restraint of trade, is to admit that, however far civilization has advanced, it has not yet eliminated a barbarous degree of selfishness; and, unfortunately, this is so!

But there must be some limitation upon that which disintegrates society; some protection to that which unites. That which raises us from the savage state cannot wholly be condemned; even though men are still so selfish as to necessitate the enforcement of police protection against the results of their cupidity.

While no more able, righteous, or legally correct opinion was ever delivered than that of Mr. Justice Harlan in the Securities case; while I doubt if we can even yet appreciate the obligations we rest under because of it (the Constitution has been subjected to enough strain in any event from the discontent of the people), I must confess that Mr. Justice Holmes in his dissent enunciates much that appeals to me as manifestly true, although, for reasons easily gatberable from this essay, I have been unable to accept his final conclusion or inference of fact in that case.

I am perfectly conscious that much in opinions of the very highest authority contradicts what I am about to say. I nevertheless and notwithstanding consider the law to be as I am striving to explain it.

Just as it is believed that "tendency" is the paramount consideration in cases of restraint, and is limited and defined by the doctrine of "indirectness," so I believe that the basis of our civilization, law, and religion is "coöperation." Though constituting the greatest source of human power for either good or evil, coöperation in turn is limited and defined by the doctrine of competition, that it may accomplish legitimate purposes only.

As to religion, I take it no one will question what I say. It would be an anomaly if a nation's law and religion were diametrically and irreconcilably in conflict on such a subject. As to our civilization, to deny this position would be equivalent to the assertion that civilization is not civilization, for civilization is coöperation among men!

And, so, to the law.

I think it is on this subject, as on the others of which I have treated, largely controlled by purpose, intent, tendency. Where men coöperate for good they are most effectively engaged in furthering the public welfare; and it is no less true that where they coöperate for evil, they in like measure intensify the evils aimed at. That I understand to be the whole doctrine of criminal conspiracy.

So, while I feel that in the Securities case the test of the stifling of all motives for competition was absolutely correct and properly applied, and while I think it has been properly applied in every case in which it has been applied by the Supreme Court; I do not think that it is by any means a universal test; and that, so far as it has been so stated as applying to all cases that must be, in the first place, limited by the case actually before the Court, and in the second place, by the fact that many exceptions have already been admitted, although the principle upon which they rest has not been formulated, the statement of the rule—though with strong dissent—still being general.

Mr. Justice Holmes forcibly says: "The provision of the statute against contracts in restraint of trade * * * does not require that all existing competitions shall be maintained. * * * The act of Congress will not be construed to mean the universal disintegration of society into single men, each at war with all the rest, or even the prevention of all further combinations for a common end. * * * A partnership is not a contract or combination in restraint of trade between the partners * * * The law, I repeat, says nothing about competition, and only prevents its suppression by contracts or combinations in restraint of trade, and such contracts or combinations derive their character as restraining trade from other features than the suppression of competition alone."

But, as has so often happened, the vindication of the opinion of the majority is found in the common law.

The extreme of the evil that the law strikes at is reached in monopoly, "sole sale;" that is, an extermination of competition. Suppression of competition is the method of accomplishing restraint universally adopted; where it is, therefore, undertaken in unusual ways or great degree, the primary presumptions against all that may restrain still needs to be negatived. In present times, to say that a suppression, an elimination of competition on a great scale, or out of the beaten and ordinary path, would not tend to oppression, would be substantially to reverse the ordinary presumption though that involves no greater hardship than the readiness to display a clean bill of health. "But if there are circumstances recited in the instrument" (or probably if they appear by averment) "it is for the court to determine whether the contract be a fair and reasonable one or not, and the test appears to be whether it is prejudicial or not to the public interest, for it is on grounds of public policy alone that these contracts are supported or avoided.

By the suppression of competition one of these magnificent combinations can, and has, filched millions of money from the people in a single year; and so, when the National police has been stricken down on his beat, is it too exacting to require that it should at least be able to establish that its purpose was not also to rob the house? To make that at least reasonably clear? Can any one say to-day that, as a rule, the stifling of competition on a great scale does not tend to raising prices, restraining trade in most cases? And if so, is the rule or exception to be proved? Is there not in such cases, just as the court has again and again said, "tendency," if not the completed injury? And where is the case that says that the provision of the statute of James as to "tendency" has ceased to be a part of the law?

But when so much is said, I feel that it will be ultimately decided that competition has thus served its full purpose; that properly used coöperation is not precluded, nor man's best friend exiled.

If it be asked, "What test must be applied to determine where coöperation may begin and competition be limited?" the answer seems clear.

Prima facie, a stifling of competition on a great scale or in unusual ways imperatively needs explanation; and the one explanation that can be safely accepted is that the greater good, "coöperation," is substituted for it; but substituted "to make," not merely "to take;" to benefit, not injure; to increase production and trade, not to limit either; to profit by more largely supplying, not denying! If that be proved, and so long as it continue, "tendency" is not present, and lawfulness continues, too! That was thought to be the Knight case!

No matter how general the language of the cases, their admitted exceptions are without intelligible explanation if this be not what the courts really mean, the underlying doctrine!

But it again only brings us back to the common law—"the exception is in furtherance of the rule."

And so we are again at our starting place. The court regards substance, not form or nomenclature. That which advances trade, plenty, happiness, is legal; that which limits or tends to limit, unlawful.

"The public have an interest in every one carrying on his trade freely; so has the individual. All interference with individual liberty of action in trading, and all restraints of trade, of themselves, if there is nothing more, are contrary to public policy and therefore void. That is the general rule. But there are exceptions. * * * It is sufficient justification, and indeed it is the only justification, if the restraint is reasonable—reasonable, that is, in reference to the interests of the parties concerned, and reasonable in reference to the interests of the public, so framed and so guarded as to afford adequate protection to the party in whose interest it is imposed, while at the same time it is in no way injurious to the public." That is the latest deliverance of one of the greatest of judges in one of the greatest two courts of the world!

A mere look at the statute books, at the decisions of the courts, at the public press, at political conventions, or any other declarations of public opinion in the last few years, must convince any one that this is not the time to relax the safeguards thrown around society by the presumption of illegality in the absence of adequate explanation, where power and interest so unite that the public may be made to contribute enormous sums to those accomplishing such union.

RESTRAINTS THROUGH INVADING LIBERTY

There are certain rights which the Constitution of the United States protects from State invasion—they are many;—but a few which it especially cherishes by protecting them from both State and individual invasion. Broadly speaking, general inherent rights are of the former class, while those which originate in the Constitution itself are alone of the latter. I am not attempting to state this with exactness, or that it may be definitely relied upon, but as a view generally and alone for another purpose. Now, while "liberty" is of the former class, liberty to engage in national trade is of the select few in the higher class coming under the direct protection of the national law, no matter by whom invaded.

While the Constitution leaves the great body of liberty to the protection of the States, except where invaded by the States, it also recognizes it as an "inalienable" right, and protects it even from the States themselves. It can, therefore, in no degree be doubted that liberty is a right of every citizen of the United States. But what is liberty? Simply "the power of election or free choice." "In this consists freedom, viz: in our being able to act or not to act as we shall choose or will. As at common law, no invasion of "free discretion," that is, liberty to engage in one's own unsold trade, is ever permitted, so under the national law even a sovereign State cannot burden National trade by withholding any part of the discretion of the owner to engage in it, even in exercise of its vital right of taxation; indeed, "if such a tax can be levied at all, its amount will rest in the discretion of the State. It is idle to say that the interests of the State would prevent oppressive taxation. Those engaged in foreign and interstate commerce are not bound to trust to its moderation in that respect; they require security."

Many and magnificent have been the opinions of the Supreme Court in defence of this right; none finer than those of Justices Harlan, Bradley,

Field, and Woods in Butchers vs. Crescent, or of Mr. Justice Peckham in Allgeyer vs. Louisiana.

No one can longer doubt that every citizen acting individually or with others has, as part of his liberty, freedom of choice as to engaging in trade. Indeed, "liberty" has recently been denominated by the Supreme Court itself as "the greatest of all rights."

But, as has been said, the right to engage in national trade emanates from and is protected by the Constitution itself and not from any State's will or grant.

It always must be remembered that it is a right arising under the Constitution itself with all that such right implies—a right that exists and that might have to be considered independently of the Sherman Act. It is manifest, therefore, that where there is a right arising from the invasion of such a right, there must be a remedy, and a remedy entirely independent of the questions of policy involved in merely contractual restraints. Possibly, indeed, independent of the Sherman Act itself. If the doctrine of Ashby vs. White is applicable to the invasion of a nationally granted right, certainly so! However this may be, a restraint of national trade, by limiting the freedom of choice as to engaging in it, must be an illegal restraint under the Sherman Act, if the restraint be involuntarily suffered.

And so it has always been held!

The subject is so completely covered by Chief Justice Fuller in Loewe vs. Lawlor, that other cases need not be referred to:

"The act prohibits any combination whatever to secure action which essentially obstructs the free flow of commerce between the States, or restricts in that regard the liberty of a trader to engage in business. The combination charged falls within the class of restraints of trade aimed at, compelling third parties and strangers involuntarily not to engage in the course of trade except on conditions that the combination imposes; and there is no doubt that (to quote the well known work of Chief Justice Erle on Trades Unions) 'at common law every person has individually, and the public also has collectively, a right to require that the course of trade should be kept free from unreasonable obstruction.'"

So it may be taken for granted that any one damaged by a conspiracy against the liberty of a citizen or corporation to engage in national trade, must be entitled to an action for that damage. And that it is in its nature simply a case of molestation at common law, involved with none of the intricacies of the subject which is being generally considered.

An important consideration in this connection is that this liberty to engage in national trade is one—perhaps the only form of liberty per se belonging to corporations, and which the States themselves cannot invade. "The power to regulate that" (interstate commerce) * * * "is the power * * * to determine when it shall be free. * * * Nor does it make any difference whether such commerce is carried on by individuals or corporations." As was said in Paul vs. Virginia: "At the time of the formation of the Constitution, a large part of the commerce of the world was carried on by corporations. The grant of power is general in its terms, making no reference to the agencies by which commerce may be carried on. It includes commerce by whomsoever conducted, whether by individuals or corporations."

DAMAGES

This not being a general treatise, but merely a consideration of certain phases, certain difficulties of the subject-matter, little need be said on the subject of damages.

One or two matters, however, may be of interest:

Great discussion has been had as to whether the damage must be to a trader, or to one in the way of his trade, or one in matters involving national trade. This subject seems free from difficulty. We are all citizens of a common country—a wrongful act prohibited, and by proper authority, and damage promised to those who suffer from that act, must be redressed! If there be, for example, a conspiracy against national trade, there can be no reason to doubt that any one injured by anything done as part of or in pursuance of that conspiracy should recover. The act expressly says so! There has been an undoubted wrong, from an assault upon national authority, and a damage from it, and there would seem to be no reason why there should not be a recovery. This question seems settled in Chattanooga vs. Atlanta.

It is, too, often absurdly argued, that if "a means" causing damage is an act within State jurisdiction, the national jurisdiction is ousted by the State's, though the act was done in pursuance of an attack on national trade; but that is practically destroying national authority altogether, as nearly every conceivable wrongful act could be redressed by the State. The Swift and Loewe cases dispose of this. In such cases this added wrong is "negligible."

One other question of great interest yet to be settled is whether the infringement of the constitutional right to pursue happiness through national trade is actionable per se, or requires proof of actual damage?

That, of course, is a mere question of policy, and depends upon the quality and importance of the right. More accurately, of whether there is such a right; for if there is, there must be an action for its invasion.

Professor Bigelow says, in his wonderful little work on "Torts," p. 26: "Speaking broadly, the cases in which it is not necessary to prove special damage in an action for tort are cases in which the act done is manifestly dangerous, so much so that instinct calls at once for redress, and would take it but for the law. Rights of life, liberty, property, and reputation furnish the subjects of such redress."

The Supreme Court has, indeed, itself regarded this right as property: "The fundamental rights to life, liberty and the pursuit of happiness, considered as individual possessions, are secured by those maxims of constitutional law which are the monuments showing the victorious progress of the race in securing to men the blessings of civilization under the reign of just and equal laws. * * * The very idea that one man may be compelled to hold his * * * means of living or any material right essential to the enjoyment of life at the mere will of another, seems to be intolerable in any country where freedom prevails, as being the essence of slavery itself."

In Aikens vs. Wisconsin, Mr. Justice Holmes says: "It is obvious that justifications may vary in extent according to the principle of policy upon which they are founded, as that while some, for instance, at common law, those affecting the use of land, are absolute, others may depend upon the end for which the act is done."

Now, if the slightest invasion of the right to enjoy land, if mere withholding of the right to sit in a chair that one owns but does not intend to use for profit, are actionable per se, what should be, what must be the policy of the law as to the unlawful interference with the highest instance of the highest form of one of the few rights granted by the national Constitution itself? The right of freedom, of election, or enjoyment of untrammeled participation in national trade?

It does seem that when the national government itself grants a right and undertakes its protection against both States and people, takes its sole protection upon itself, and declares it of the highest importance, it should warrant at least as high a sanction of policy as the right to sit in a chair from which nothing but mere comfort is intended or expected. In re Debs, illustrates how determined the Supreme Court has been to safeguard this right! But the analogies, if not the absolute decisions, seem to cover this question. Indeed, it has been long settled that the dignity of the sovereignty prevents it admitting that its grants are so valueless that they can be invaded without reparation in every case. "Generally speaking, every willful interference with a franchise is actionable without regard to the defendant's act being done in good faith by reason of a mistaken notion of duty or claim of right, or being consciously wrongful. 'If a man hath a franchise and is hindered in the enjoyment thereof an action doth lie, which is an action upon the case. Holt, C. J."

But that liberty itself, especially that emanating from the sovereign, is put upon still higher grounds, is clear.

The opinion of Lord Camden—a landmark in the history of our liberty—in 1763, in Huckle vs. Money, is instructive! And this is followed in Scott vs. Donald, which, if rightly comprehended, covers the exact point now being discussed.

There the officers of the State of South Carolina had interfered with this exact right, or liberty, and had withheld a few dollars' worth of liquors being obtained through interstate trade. Action was brought for this invasion of the nationally granted right, and six thousand dollars of damages claimed; but as the liquors detained were of so little value, the question of jurisdiction was raised, because the amount in controversy did not reach two thousand dollars, as required by the Act, but the Supreme Court said: "The intentional, malicious, and repeated interference by the defendants with the exercise of personal rights and privileges secured to the plaintiff by the Constitutiontion of the United States * * * constitutes, as we think, a wrong and injury not the subject of compensation by a mere money standard, but fairly within the doctrine where exemplary damages have been allowed." And the court held that for this invasion of such a right the jury would have been entitled to give a verdict for the full amount claimed, which, being six thousand dollars, of course bore no relation to the few dollars of mere property actually involved. Indeed, so far as the exercise of liberty in relation to national trade is concerned, it is peculiarly close in analogy to the cases of franchises, which have always been held to be governed by the rule of policy applicable to real and personal property— only in this case the sanctions behind protection are peculiarly high. For the right to engage in national trade is a franchise, whether secured to individuals or corporations, emanating not from the common law, but the Constitution itself—the supreme law of the land!

THE KNIGHT CASE

Whatever the crimes perpetrated in the name of "liberty," they are not a circumstance to those sought to be justified by the opinion of Chief Justice Fuller in United States vs. Knight.

And yet, that was perhaps the most ably argued of all the trust cases, and resulted in two of the most learned opinions—those of the Chief Justice and of Mr. Justice Harlan—to be found in the reports. Indeed, in the one or the other of those opinions can be found the foundation of most of the doctrines that have been enunciated since.

And, what is striking, is that, so far as the law was concerned, the difference of opinion was negligible.

The difficulty was not that the Chief Justice did not know the law of the case, but that he knew so much more than some of his readers—certainly this one—that he assumed understanding where instruction might be needed.

The Supreme Court says in Arkansas vs. Bank: "Whether the Supreme Court was warranted in assuming the facts, as it sets them forth, is no concern of ours. The important thing is that it was at pains to state them, and that it can have had no purpose in doing so other than to establish a liability. * * * If the statute imposed liability without, etc., * * * there was no need to go into these details."

If this be the right method of approach, and, of course, it is, being pointed out by the Supreme Court, there should be no difficulty as to the Knight case.

In the Knight case, the purpose being to prove non-liability, only those facts were necessarily inquired into whose presence would create liability, if found.

As the meaning of the decision, therefore, absolutely depends upon these findings, let us seek it in them.

In the first place, it was thought necessary to find that there was a complete purchase, a complete change of property. The reason is obvious.

In the second, that every one was left free. Again the reason is obvious.

In the third, that it was a case of contract, and the provisions related solely to that purchase and not to subsequent arrangements as to trade. Again the reason is obvious.

Again, that the refineries had continued to operate and had actually increased their product, that the object of purchase "was manifestly private gain in the manufacture of the commodity;" "that there was nothing in the proofs to indicate any intention to put a restraint upon trade or commerce" and, finally, that what was done was either "sanctioned," or "permitted" "by the States of residence or creation." And the decision—a veritable mine of law—held, of course correctly, that, under these findings, the restraint was indirect and, therefore, lawful.

Let the converse of this be stated:

If there had been invasion of liberty, proof of intention to restrain national trade, the control of discretion as to a business not completely owned, unified or merged, the deprivation of the public of a great utility for supplying a necessary food; a purpose to profit by non use, by stifling competition, instead of through production, acts prohibited by the States of creation or residence as in violation of their public policy as well as tending to a diminution of National trade—what then? The later cases fully answer. There would have been "tendency," direct restraint, illegality! And, if the method of approach now adopted (and it has the Supreme Court's sanction) be correct, that is what the Knight case decides!

It is the present purpose to demonstrate this. There has been a tendency to criticise the findings of the Knight case, especially that relating to intention or tendency—the sequel has unquestionably justified Mr. Justice Harlan's fears in that respect. But it is not fair to judge any case by conditions of trade arising or acts committed after the decision has been rendered. For the present purposes, it may not be important whether the inferences of fact were correct or not, but it well illustrates the law to consider them. Indeed, were they not the inferences universally drawn before the trusts had debauched trade to accomplish crime? Why was a man permitted to covenant that he would protect a good-will that he had sold? Simply because every one, for centuries, had considered that the best way of insuring that the business would go on; would maintain, or increase trade. No one had thought that a man would invest capital in a business that he might destroy it. Just a few months before the Knight case this subject had been carefully considered by the House of Lords itself, and a similar conclusion reached. If, therefore, the inference was unjustifiable in the one case, neither of the greatest tribunals of the world was correct, and the

Supreme Court had the justification of the precedent just set by the House of Lords.

The importance of the findings that "the manifest object" was to profit by use, not abuse, by manufacture, not restraint, can be understood when it is remembered that the Chief Justice was professedly writing the opinion "in the light of the common law," and concluding that all that was done was "sanctioned" by it. The great decision upon that law, with which the Chief Justice was of course perfectly familiar, was Oregon vs. Winsor. There, too, an instrumentality had been changed from one owner to another, and the transfer had also been held "sanctioned," "permitted," but why? The answer to this covers the whole subject. Simply because it "had no tendency to destroy the usefulness of the steamer, and did not deprive the country of any industrial agency. The transaction merely transferred the steamer from the employment of one company to that of another, situated and doing business in another State. It involved no * * * cessation or diminution of its business whatever. The presumption is that the arrangement * * * promoted the general interests of commerce. * * * The public was not injured by being deprived of any of the ness enterprise of the country. * * * The vendees did not incapacitate themselves from carrying on business just as they had previously done and in the same locality. * * * The vendees did not incapacitate themselves from carrying on business. * * * Their business was rather facilitated by the arrangement." It is impossible that the Chief Justice had not this decision in mind as he had shortly before expressly followed it in Gibbs vs. Gas Company, where he himself says: "It is also too well settled to admit of doubt that a corporation cannot disable itself by contract from performing the public duties which it has undertaken and by agreement compel itself to make public accommodation or convenience subservient to its private interests." In view of all this, it is absolutely impossible to say that he was finding that it was lawful and "sanctioned" by the States, or any of them, to deprive the country of its industrial agencies, to destroy business, stop commerce and production, that national trade might be limited and the profits of monopoly be swollen!

No State ever sanctioned such public evil, and no judge ever knew this better than the Chief Justice. The whole case manifestly turned on the careful findings of its facts: the fact that the purpose was to profit by production, not by restraining commerce either directly or indirectly. For otherwise, the question of "indirection" could not possibly have been raised at all, since complete lawfulness is its very foundation.

This can, however, fortunately now be demonstrated by two later opinions of the Chief Justice. No sooner had this decision been rendered than it was promptly abused by the trusts; and, after awhile, the Securities case, identical in method, came before the court, and it then found "tendency" as a fact on its added knowledge of trust methods, but it really followed the law of the Knight case, departing only from its inference of fact, which the trusts bad proved no longer tenable, by their subsequent misconduct.

And this is established by the unanimous opinion in the Harriman case. There Chief Justice Fuller says: "The objection was that the exercise of its powers, whether those of owner or of trustee, would tend to prevent competition, and thus to restrain commerce. Some of our number thought that as the Securities Company owned the stock the relief sought could not be granted, but the conclusion was that the possession of the power which, if exercised, would prevent competition, brought the case within the statute, no matter what the tenure of title was."

That is "tendency" controlled; not the question as to whether that unlawful thing resulted from one form of forbidden thing, rather than from another. But if this be not sufficient demonstration that the Knight case turned on the innocence of intent then believed in, Loewe vs. Lawlor certainly must close the discussion, for the Chief Justice again expressly says, p. 297:

"We do not pause to comment on cases such as United States vs. Knight (156 U. S. 1), Hopkins vs. United States (171 U. S. 578), and Anderson vs. United States, in which the undisputed facts showed that the purpose of the agreement was not to obstruct or restrain interstate commerce. The object and intention of the combination determined its legality." And that is a better summary of the decision in the Knight case than any of its critics has ever reached; and, what is better still, it is the conclusion that the whole history of the law requires!

INTRA-STATE ACTS

So far as criminal liability under the Act is concerned, intra-state acts are only important as evidence tending to prove the interstate offence. The making of the combination, etc., is in and of itself the offence; and nothing further need be said on this phase of the matter.

But where a recovery under the Seventh Section is sought, they become of great importance; indeed, they may be vital.

The Act was manifestly drawn by a masterhand, as is shown in many respects.

As an example, acts in restraint must be of two or more; there must be some combined action. It was not overlooked that, otherwise, everyone who did not use his property, or stopped using his property to its full working capacity, might find himself subject to suits and penalties.

But the strongest illustration of the legal knowledge and precise and proper use of words of the drafters of the Act is found in this Seventh Section: "Any person who shall be injured in his business or property * * * may sue therefore * * * and shall recover threefold the damages by him sustained," etc. No one not an able lawyer could have drawn that section, for it exactly follows the principles of the common law.

The right to sue is, as at common law, made dependent not upon damage at all, but upon "injury"; that is, "injuria," which, in turn, is "invasion of legal rights"; "obstruction," or "hindrance," as Lord Holt would have called it.

But at common law, as Broom says (Maxims) at p. 157: "Although damnum absque injuria is a matter of frequent occurrence, yet injuria absque damno may be said to be unknown to our law; for 'a damage is not merely pecuniary, but an injury imports a damage when a man is thereby hindered of his right.' Per Holt, C. J. Ashby vs. White, 2 Ld. Raym. 955." This is finely stated by Lord Esher, M. R., in Campanhia vs. British (1892), 2 Q. B., at p. 405: "Damages," he says, "cannot be asked for as being themselves a cause of action. No one can seek damages on the bare assertion that he is entitled to damages, and therefore claims damages. Damage is sometimes stated to be a cause of action, but then damage means injury. Damages are one of the reliefs asked for as the compensation for an injury. But then the injury is the cause of action." Which is almost a paraphrase of the Act!

The fundamental, the original purpose of damages was the preservation, the vindication of the enjoyment of rights; that is, of liberty itself; and, thus, arose the necessity of the constitutional right and provision guaranteeing a trial by jury in civil cases; for juries were always considered by freemen as the best appraisers of the value of that intangible thing called li (illegible text) pon which, however, the value and enjoym (illegible text) tangible things must ultimately dep (illegible text) o one but a jury has any constitutiona (illegible text) fix them in an action for tort. Watt vs. Watt, (1905), A. C. 120.

The framer of the Act must, therefore, have understood this, and in giving the action for the "injuria," not the mere pecuniary "damage," he not only made the Act conform with the general theory of the common law, but brought it within its liberty-protecting principles.

But he went further—following the Statute of James I, and knowing that in all cases the injury imports some damages, he provides that, in this case, for the better protection of trade, that damages, or any damage, shall be threefold.

This being all so, it follows that, as no action is given in the absence of "injuria," the Act positively contemplates and requires that some right, either at common or statutory law, or under the Constitution, must be obstructed or hindered by some part or act of the conspiracy, andc., to justify a suit under this statute.

But that means, and must mean, that two things are absolutely necessary to found a civil action. First, that two or more have combined in restraint of trade, or one or more have attempted to monopolize; and, second, that through that combination, or attempt, or some act a part of it, the plaintiff has been hindered in some right. Damage alone will not do; its absence alone is also not a defence.

This is well expressed in Rourke vs. Elk, 75 N. Y. App. Div., at p. 148.

This, then, brings us to the subject matter of this chapter.

As national and constitutional rights are, if not entirely, at least chiefly, the liberty or right to enjoy other rights; and as those other rights are, as we have already explained, also chiefly, if not entirely, protected by and within State jurisdiction, an action for damage must, in practically every case, involve that which is both interstate and intra-state.

In other words, the object, or the intent, must be to invade national right; but the means equally must, almost of necessity, be some intra-state matter.

Nothing could be more thoroughly intra-state than the specific transactions described in Atlanta vs. Chattanooga, 203 U. S. 390.

Whilst our objects, our purposes, may be interstate, they must almost inevitably be achieved chiefly, if not entirely, through intra-state acts and things.

It is of the first importance to bear this in mind, as otherwise error cannot be avoided.

Take the Knight case, for example. There the object was to profit by manufacture, not by curtailing trade. It was held perfectly legal to control a number of Pennsylvania refineries with this object, though manufacture could not be carried on except through imports of raw sugars. In the Addyston case, it quite as much related to the control of manufactures, even, indeed, to a less control; but as, under the circumstances, it was fair to presume that the object was to lessen competition and thus restrain trade, it was unanimously held to be illegal; and just so in the Montague and the Loewe cases. Some control of manufactures was sought in each case; but the legality of that control was determined by the purpose, the object of that control, ascertained, of course, from its real tendency under the circumstances. Thus, in both the Knight and Montague cases, import into a State was a necessity of the business; but, as in the former the "manifest object" was to do the business, and thus probably increase imports, it was held to be legal, an indirect restraint; whilst in the latter, as the purpose was to curtail the plaintiff's business, it was held to be a direct and, therefore, illegal restraint of that interstate trade which was a necessary incident of it.

And it must be so in each case.

All things are of necessity within the States, and are all subject to State jurisdiction; and the national jurisdiction does not attach, cannot attach, until, or unless, a use of them is intended against nationally protected right; but when that intent, that object is once reasonably inferred from the natural and real tendency of what is done, the national jurisdiction is as firmly established as that of the State was primarily.

The manufacture of rifles must be a purely State matter; but those who manufacture them with the object of shooting every one who dares exercise his freedom to trade between two States, would find the national jurisdiction reached him, notwithstanding every rifle was made in a single State, and as a purely intra-state matter.

No doubt the Debs riots in Chicago were a local offence, committed in each separate instance within a State, but their reasonable results being to stop national trade, the Supreme Court found no difficulty in stopping them. In re Debs, 158 U. S. 564.

Since, therefore, an inv~ion of a right which, in almost every conceivable case must be an intra-state right, is a necessity of an action under the Act, the argument that it is a defence to an action where the prohibited combination or attempt is properly inferred that intra-state matters are involved is absurd, however constantly made.

Where there is the "dangerous probability," constituting tendency, the "object," the "intent," to invade national right, the fact that that object includes, and is furthered by intra-state matters is, as Chief Justice Fuller points out in Loewe vs. Lawlor, 208 U. S. 274, "negligible"; and this is as clearly pointed out in the Swift case, 196 U. S., at p. 397, and even before that in Montague vs. Lowry, 193 U. S. 38. And should require no further discussion!

CONCLUSIONS AND CONCLUSION

If the theories herein advanced are correct, they should accord with and reconcile the cases, at least those in the Supreme Court.

The Knight case has been examined. It was decided "in the light" of such cases as Oregon vs. Winsor, and the Maxim case. When businesses were bought to add to prosperity, not to stifle competition; when the manifest purpose was only so to profit; when the trust was actually increasing product to fill the channels of trade; and before the real policy of buying productive agencies only to withdraw them from public service, although by those already having enormous capacity idle, was inaugurated by the trusts. The Chief Justice was right because he saw; Mr. Justice Harlan because he foresaw. But with "intent," "interest" and "tendency" in its legal sense added, the decision in the Securities case was a legal necessity of the Knight case, its legitimate offspring; though the misconduct of the trusts had even then only convinced a majority of the court of the extent of individual wrong-doing!

The Joint Traffic and Freight Association cases are likewise beyond criticism. The circuit courts and circuit courts of appeals had largely been misled by Mr. Justice Jackson's exceedingly able but very misleading opinion In re Greene. He there had said:

"The question of its (a contract's) reasonableness depends on the consideration whether it is more injurious to the public than is required to afford a fair protection to a party in whose favor it is secured."

And a complete misunderstanding of such cases as Mogul vs. McGregor. It had never been common law that the public might be "reasonably" robbed a little, if the malefactor but profited a great deal. That, as had always been the case, was directly contrary to the law. Judge Taft, Justice Harlan and Judge Lurton concurring, made this, at last, clear in the Addyston case, saying:

"In Mallen vs. May, Baron Parke said: 'Contracts for the partial restraint are upheld, not because they are advantageous to the individual with whom the contract is made, and a sacrifice pro tanto of the rights of the community, but because it is for the benefit of the public at large that they should be enforced.' Many of these partial restraints on trade are perfectly consistent with public convenience and the general interest and have been supported. Such is the case of the disposing of a shop in a particular place, with a contract on the part of the vendor not to carry on a trade in the same place. It is, in effect, the sale of a good-will, and offers an encouragement to trade," etc.

That so valuable a case as Mogul vs. McGregor should not only have been totally misunderstood, but completely misapplied by the lower courts is almost incomprehensible. For it is the star case for, not against, competition. The lower courts seem to have completely overlooked the fact that such arrangements though made unlawful in all senses by the Sherman Act, were only unlawful in the sense that they would not be enforced— would be treated as nude pacts at common law. However much the parties might proclaim their servitude, the common law simply contented itself by continuing to regard them as free.

But, since the ultimate end in the Mogul case was to restrain trade, though through the legal means of competition, the combination was held in the sense of non-enforceability to be illegal—not legal at all! The difficulty for the plaintiffs in that case, and the sole difficulty, was that, having no Sherman Act, they had to show illegality in means to make it a case of molestation; and without molestation they could not recover damages, for there was no legal "injuria;" and they could but allege savage and unreasonable competition, and see how splendidly they were answered.

Lord Bowen, in the greatest English opinion on this subject, says: "The truth is that the combination of capital for the purposes of trade and competition (what was thought to be the case in the Greene and the Knight cases) "is a very different thing from the combinations of several against one with a view to harm him as falls under the head of an indictable conspiracy. There is no just cause or excuse in the latter class of cases. There is such a just cause or excuse in the former. * * * To limit combinations of capital when used for purposes of competition * * * would, in the present day, be impossible—would be only another method of attempting to set boundaries to the tides." Which is just the view contended for! To combine to add all the benefits of cooperation to all of those safeguarded by competition, cannot, possibly, be a public evil; but nevertheless the courts have a right and duty to, and do, in the first instance examine each such case critically. The remarks on this decision in the Addyston case should remove all further misunderstanding of it.

Perhaps, after all, it is fortunate that the Supreme Court refused to examine it or the common law critically in the two cases under consideration. For by so doing it has given the common law the tremendous added sanction afforded by like results reached by the independent reasonings of powerful minds. The dissent in those cases is quite as interesting as the prevailing opinions, as it but fortifies the right conclusion.

Mr. Justice White most ably argues along the lines of Mr Justice Jackson—that contracts that reasonably restrained were not contracts properly called contracts in restraint at all; and so were not within the act; but the fallacy of this seems to be in the fact that every contract that really restrained trade itself (and not merely the conduct of a trader that trade might be encouraged by honest dealing) was held to be unreasonable and unlawful, so that "reasonable restraints" were restraints that did not restrain at all, and only "reasonable" because they did not restrain! But it was not the common law, nor is it "reasonable" to say that a restraint is not a restraint because it is a reasonable restraint, while it is both to say "we shall look at substance not names, and if we find a thing is an encouragement we shall not treat it as a resstraint, no matter what it is called. The strange part of the dissent is that there is much in it to prove that Mr. Justice White really had the true distinction in his mind all the while. He even cites Mr. Justice Maule in Rannie vs. Irvine.

The passage in the Freight Association case on the treatment of intent, should be noted, being of the utmost importance, as are the following illustrations of what may be a direct restraint from the Joint Traffic Association case: "There can be no doubt that the general tendency of competition among competing railroads is toward lower rates for transportation, and the result of lower rates is generally a greater demand for the articles so transported, and this greater demand can only be gratified by a larger supply, the furnishing of which increases commerce. * * * The natural, direct and immediate effect of competition is, however, to lower rates, and to thereby increase the demand for commodities, the supplying of which increases commerce, and an agreement, whose first and direct effect is to prevent this play of competition restrains instead of promoting trade and commerce." And, of course, identity of reasoning must apply where one of the steps between the act and the result is removed, as where manufacture itself is stopped, and it was so unanimously determined in the Addyston case. Since this, there has been little difficulty. The Montague case was of a class where recovery has always been allowed, for citizens' freedom as to national trade was limited. It in no way conflicts with the Anderson case, where there was neither tendency nor intent to that effect. The Hopkins case is of the same class as the Anderson.

The Securities case has already been sufficiently noted. It really largely turned, as did the Knight case, upon an inference as to the fact of tendency;

but trade had so changed as to demand a new finding on that score in the later case.

One thing that is puzzling, however, in the opinion of Mr. Justice White, may be noticed. Pollock, C. B., in the Egerton case, says: "Where a contract is directly opposed to public welfare, it is void, though the parties may have a real interest in the matter, and an apparent right to deal with it." That has certainly been the accepted doctrine. Now, if "sole sale," or that tending to it, were the evils aimed at, the evils that constituted illegality in any contract tending to it, what earthly difference in principle does it make that the contract is made in one form rather than another? Every justice agreed that the contract in the Addyston case concerning admitted rights of property of the parties was illegal, because it tended to restrain trade; then why not any other form of contract that tended to the same evil? What special form of sanctity has a sale as contrasted with any other evil contract? Sales in all directions had been limited where tending to evil, and for centuries, and without doubt! With trade as it has since been conducted, the tendency in the Knight sales has been demonstrated to be as deadly as the sale of discretion in the Addyston. Would it not be strange, then, that form alone should be considered of the slightest importance, and is not the true explanation that "sales" had taken on this sacred hue solely because for centuries they had never before been abused? Is there any other logical or sensible explanation? But a man has no unlimited right to sell poisons, and it can make no difference whether the poison was to kill men or kill that trade upon which their lives, comfort, and happiness so largely depend. The truth is, that the trusts have placed what was an unmixed agency for good among the most dangerous instruments of evil, and the courts have ultimately become conscious of the change; and that is the sole difference in the Knight and Securities cases.

It must never be forgotten that "when the acts consist of making a combination calculated to cause temporal damage, the power to punish such acts, when done maliciously, cannot be denied, because they are to be followed and worked out by conduct which might have been lawful if not preceded by the acts. No conduct has such an absolute privilege as to justify all possible schemes of which it may be a part. The most innocent and constitutionally protected of acts or omissions may be made a step in a criminal plot, and if it is a step in a plot neither its innocence nor the Constitution is sufficient to prevent the punishment of the plot by law." That sales for immoral or illegal uses are illegal has long been settled.

Such an attempt as this, made by one long withdrawn from practice, and accomplished during a single day's vacation, must necessarily be crude, fragmentary and incomplete. But believing that the common law has received its greatest vindication; that the charge of inconsistency in the decisions of the Supreme Court is unjust and answered by considering that common law; that however little value my own conclusions may have, they may at least have some place as suggestions to those whose opinions have weight and value, I have felt justified in submitting my thoughts, knowing that it can do no harm, and hoping that it may do a little good.

Another consideration that must not be lost sight of, and that warrants every citizen's earnest consideration of this subject, is its danger to our splendid form of government. If that have a unique superiority, it is that ultimate power is vested in a body of men who but decide—not use. Tendency to selfish application is therefore reduced as it has never been in any other country. The keeping of that power there should, therefore, be the highest object of every lover of his country. But all history, from the Roman Emperors down, but demonstrates that any power under which monopolies spring to life or flourish is doomed. Never was Rhinegold so fatal to its possessors. What Zeno, what the absolute Tudors and Stuarts could not maintain in ignorant and despotic ages, can be no less a danger to any modern institution. Fortunately, the common law, and the Sherman Act interpreted by it, require no protection of monopolies by the Supreme Court in their enforcement of law; and it is fortunate and cannot be too well understood, as, were it required, it would inevitably destroy the most important and essential feature of our free government—America's greatest invention in government!

www.ingramcontent.com/pod-product-compliance
Lightning Source LLC
Chambersburg PA
CBHW071637170526
45166CB00003B/1358